Pet

KELLA HANNA-WAYNE

the Journey
from Abuse
to Recovery

Printed in the United States of America
First Printing, 2022
Yopp! Publishing
United States
www.yoppvoice.com

Acknowledgements

Many thanks to the following publications in which some of these poems first appeared:

Two in the Morning: *Cast Macabre;* Stupid Bitch, Breath of Who we Could Be, Black Flyers: *The Cynic;* Date Night: *Black Petals;* A Better Place, The Turn, Oregon Coast, Cotton, Date Night: *Capella Market Employee Art Exhibit;* Pin-Prick: *Hello Horror;* How Could She Stay With Him?: *Architrave Press.*

Editing:
Katherine Grace; Amy, Jessica, & Hazel of The Blueprint System

Cover Art:
Kella Hanna-Wayne, AJ, & The Blueprint System

Publisher:
Yopp!

*For Amy, Sylvia,
Susan, & Casey.*

Forward

The goal of this book has always been to make the feelings that result from abuse and its aftermath as concrete and real as possible to whoever chooses to read it. As such, reading this book involves having an openness to those feelings. This is a gentle acknowledgement that this poetry includes graphic descriptions of sexual violence, domestic violence, and self-harm, both real and metaphorical, as well as imagery of violence by firearm. I encourage you to read it with a safe environment and self-compassion at your disposal, but I do encourage you to read it. I promise that if you reach the end, we'll both come out the other side, in tact and whole.

Contents

Cotton

you told me not to say bad things about you

but somehow I couldn't

every good word I said
twisted out of my grasp
became a bad one
that is all they heard

to stop my words from turning on you
I took cotton balls
stuffed them down my throat

all my words
got caught in cotton
built up
of you
I said little

you're gone
the cotton and the words
still in my throat
whenever I speak of you
the words won't come

Part I

Repression

Submissive

you see the rebellion on my face

down on my knees
you press my face
into your sweaty lap
shortening my breath
till I cry, till I give in

struggling to shrink
to be a shining shell

clean your counter, these dishes
cook, sweep, smile, massage

go hungry

in a weak moment
I risk feeling
I can't shove myself
in this box   anymore

you throw me to the street
in my heels and nylons
my thoughts broadcast across my forehead
the wrong tone, a word
something I say gives me away

when you call
and grant me a second chance
I'll come
but I pray that next time
I'll let go of myself

no conscious soul
can do what you ask

Target

I've covered the places
that are most vulnerable
you can't have them till I say so

it makes you angry
you take aim at my skin
shoot me full of meteor holes
across my chest, down my legs
tell me to give it up

all of my body
should be yours

I don't surrender

you rip from me
what I hold back
keep it behind you
where I can't reach

my empty body lies pinned
under you
you've taken me
given nothing

Played

my friends fall away
like hand-carved pieces
on your chessboard
you gently tip over
one by one leaving me
alone and vulnerable

As I try to flee across
the empty marble expanse
I could swear you move
your pieces and mine
it's more than a defeat
if I help you win

Ghost Lines
Act 1

Sir:	When I say, "Good girl," I want you to say, "Thank you sir."
Pet:	Yes, sir.
Sir:	Good girl.
Pet:	Thank you, sir.

Pet:	Sir, there is a problem that requires your attention.
Sir:	If you're gonna do this, do it right, Pet.
Pet:	Okay, I'm sorry sir.
Pet:	Sir, may I speak with you?
Sir:	I guess.
Pet:	Sir, there is a problem that requires your attention. If it's not too much trouble, I'd appreciate your assistance very much.
Sir:	Fine. What's the problem, pet?

Pet:	Here's what you asked for, sir.
Sir:	I guess you don't really want to be here.
Pet:	I'm sorry, sir?
Sir:	This is it? This is the money you're going to give me?
Pet:	Yes, sir, that's all that was left.

Sir: You really expect me to believe that it cost that
          much? I didn't think you'd steal, Pet, not from
          me.

Pet: I didn't! I promise!

Sir: [silence]

Sir: I think you decided you'd rather go home than
          stay here with me and get better.

Pet: No, sir. I want to get better. I want to stay.

          Please don't make me go.

Promise

I face the wood panels
trying to wrap my head around
where I went wrong

I once promised myself
in a solid part of me

you've been a bad girl
turn around

if a man ever hit me

you need to be punished

he would lose me
no question

when you spank me

savage stinging
once, twice
three times
no safeword

I do not move
I plead to the walls
for strength I do not have

Pet

what can they think
when they see me

tight silk skirt
four inch heels
lacy bra, plunging neckline
long rips in my nylon stockings

every week
I come with heaps of laundry
cotton boxers
denim jeans that could
swallow me whole

every week
handfuls of quarters
sticky with detergent
only $1.50 per wash
$1.25 on Tuesdays

every week
before I leave
I carefully fold each item
hot from the dryer

no one speaks to me

perhaps they see my leash
snaking across the tiles
trailing out the door

I am surely not far
from my owner

Two in the Morning

get out of bed
re-dress, the way he likes it
put on your coat
slowly kill yourself

your skin is vulnerable in night air
the world has begun to close over you
the awareness gets heavier and heavier
until your body can't hold it
pretend to go back to sleep

parts of you have begun to fall off
ears, fingers
a shoulder, a breast
they litter the path to his house

knock on the door
your heart pounding
knowing your lover is waiting
a gun in hand

spread your broken body for him
and shut your eyes
before the bullet leaves the gun

Deadened

I wrap my arms and legs
in muslin
thinking of you
with every layer

I weave a sheet of the thoughts
you've given me
I'm glad that I gave you
my chance at survival
all the money I had
placed my hope in your hands

I paint the fabric with your symbols
wind it thickly
about my eyes

I am padded so thoroughly
it feels like a lover's touch

I think not
of the servants of Egypt
who wrapped their kings in golden cloth
hoping to forget the grief inside

Pin-Prick

for you, I sew my hand
into a piece of mending
the silver point
pokes through the fabric
pierces my finger tip
emerges below my nail

a straight stitch
through five fleshy digits
a clean pattern, like a star

the thread wiped clean
with a bloody rag
I continue along my arm
the outer seams of my body

covered in tiny holes
I can't understand

why my heart won't let me sleep

Good Girl

my head's impaled
deeper than I want to go
you keep your hands
on my head
hold me down

I struggle, gasping for air
trying to come up
you're crammed down my throat
I gag

your hands glide along my shoulders

I'm trapped in time
in this movement
long past exhaustion

you grip my hair
press into me hard
demand my obedience

I surrender
mucus spit
tears

you always come when I cry
and then your hands
disappear

Breath of Who We Could Be

I don't remember
what lead up to it
why we were suddenly
laid bare

making love
so unexpected
our rough edges chafing

love me, I said
I love you, I love you
I love you
you said

words
surrendered
for a moment

Ashes

late at night
I give you a last massage
brush your hair in darkness
give you the presence
and warmth of my body
I almost fall asleep
as if we are two regular lovers

this is when I know
it's time for me to withdraw
to my own stiff pallet on the couch

to sleep alone
with my smoldering hopes

Reach

"I don't know what you're talking about. My records show that I've paid you back everything I owe. You need to stop texting me. Your rent is not my problem and I can't talk to you when you're like this."

help

my friend
answers

she talks relationships
power dynamics
the future
she is the first
who does not talk about you

"I can lend you the money" she says
"that's no problem,

but do you know what do *you* want?"

churning
then rippling
my very own thoughts
are   new   and   slow

they fill me up like gas
soon they take up more space

                              than I do

The Only Constant Is...

"are you sure you don't
want to see the ducklings?"

a memory
of the soft tender being
trembling
in my hand
"no," I reply
"I remember the old ducklings"

"those ones? they grew up,
some of them went into pots!"

he watches me for signs of shock
and is pleased to find them

I ask
how can he reconcile
the image of life in his hands
with duck and vegetable stew
I like to pretend it didn't happen

"I can't be in denial
about anything," he says.

I notice the veils that cloud his eyes

Stupid Bitch

you hand me this name
insist it suits me

I try to put it on
drape it over my shoulders-
tie it around my waist-
put one leg in at a time-
frown
I cannot

it does not fit

The Door

you know your hold on me is weakening
the last time I tried to leave
I almost didn't come back

my words fly over you
like scraps of paper
you say the best thing for me right now
is to slam my prison door shut

you were the one who opened the door for me
brought me to the world outside
showed me grass and sun for the first time

but you say I must return
or you'll abandon us for good

no, not again
I can't go back
not all four walls no way to climb out trapped forever
again

I close the door

███████████████████████ *boom*

and scream

every
moment
hurts

movement

thought

escape...

your eyes fall on me
full of blame
so heavy

my head cannot hold it all

my legs are moving
my coat is in my hand
I can't remember how I got here
I am leaving

you shoot words like bees
they sting, disappear
I've forgotten them already

you think you are freeing me
that you're still in charge

stars whirl over head
shifting

no I am leaving you

Part II

Recovery

Dark Side

when I step into the space
that is not yours
I hear a call go out

dark eddies
slither up my legs
taking pleasure in my return

they've been waiting
in the shadows
for me to join them

I gather each one in my arms
hold them close
as they burrow into my heart

I inhale sinful air
knowing your door is closed
and I'm glad

Diary Entry

but what if I fucked things up

what if I'm seeing
what I want to and I'm
corrupt
and selfish

I really miss you
everything you did was for my own good
I should be with you now
and I'm not
because I can't handle it

I'm too weak

if-

if you were just using me-

but what if everything was my fault
and I just don't want it to have been

Love Sick

at night
in the folds of my heart
a crack opens

seeping
acidic liquid
stinging
my wet interior
hissing

whispering

I miss you

The Turn

always looking for the sun
I got lost

when we first met
I could tell by the color of your hair
gold inside and out
you knew the sun intimately
you promised me we'd see it

in a sky so large
I saw it
a fire belly
just above the sea
I loved you for leading me there

you turned my path
away from the sun
you pushed me toward
the blue glass beneath

you lead me into the shallows
deepening until the tide
crashed over my body

you never told me
that in order to reach
the sun
I had to drown

Ghost Lines
Act 2

I wrote it all down
on paper
so I wouldn't forget

no that's not right
you wrote it for me
because I could never get it right

you said, when you have a problem
you say those words
and I said yes sir thank you sir

I kept the paper in my purse
I memorized it
I said it right

I tried to find the paper today
I wanted proof that it really happened
to feel it between my fingers

but I don't know where I put it
I lost the piece of paper
the words are gone

Trigger

wiping pans
hot from the oven
I burn myself

white shock
starting in my fingers
shoots up my arms
through my heart
lightning to my brainstem

after several breaths
I reach again for the pan

but an echo
sounds
in my body

the risk of reprise

my hands tremble
stopped

Confrontation

how can I
poke holes in you
reach the oh-so-fragile
pink flesh

what insult
will tear you down
force you to bow to me
creature of weakness

what scorn can I give back
that will not be reversed
so I avoid being transformed
into what you think I am

cornered
how can I leave
unscathed

Like I Did

you used to wonder loudly
why are broken women
so attracted to me?
why can't I find someone healthy?

looking now with new eyes
I can see the villain in you
and the weakness in me

I wonder too
if the next girl
has already fallen
for your empathy
like I did

if I am already on your list
of malevolent exes

if you'll tell her I'm crazy
just like all the others

if she'll believe you

like I did

when she meets me
will she only see my darkness?
will she find strength
where I did not?
will my light find her
and prove to her once and for all
that you were wrong?

The Mirror

the first time I meet her
I think she looks just like me
as if I hope you still love me

she and I look into each others eyes
a lacquered mirror dissolves between us
we can touch each other
take words out of each others mouths

our hands once twisted the same door handle
the hanging decoration that I made
she quietly admired after I was gone

her eyes are dark and beautiful
and I hear my voice in hers

against our will
we were taken
to the same hidden dimension

our search
for the way out
is the same

We Who Know

you are exiled from yourself
living on the outskirts
prowling borders
the dark city
of an abandoned soul

hollow as you are
you look to your lovers
to fill you
you hate us for being people
un-severed and complete

you'll only become more brittle
shed all that you can
attempting to expel the force inside
that banishes you

with no substance left within
we know
you will someday fall

Blades

that old mix of poisons
hate and lust
tear through my veins

seeing you again
you back me up
against a wall

body pressed against mine
knife at my throat
you dare me to speak

I want to taste
poison in my body
once more

I glint
with steel of my own
you see me answer
yes I dare

Every Mistake

sometimes when I wash dishes
I smell a hint of soap
and I am at your house again

dim light, hot and sweaty
whir of a fan

the longer I take
on this single dish
the larger the number
I will write out on the notepad

the yellow pencil stub
I mustn't break
the mysterious calculations
you've written for me
the amount at the bottom
you'll pay me
in my own money

money I need to pay rent
buy food

money I will return to you
if I don't wash dishes
with a smile on my face
if I don't do them well enough

when not if
I make my next mistake

sometimes I think I never left

Part III

Retrospect

Black Flyers

the moment before I say I love you
a storm cloud descends on my body

the darkness is so close
I can't see the space
before my eyes
the air crackles
with the promise of lightning
and dry rain
drenches my face

words trembling in my chest
I'm afraid the snipers
will shoot through
the folds of darkness
shatter each syllable
into pieces too small to hold

the longer I hide
in deafening emptiness
the closer they come

the words fly without breath
the air clears
I give you the storm

each time I touch you
I can feel it still

Persuasion

I'm unaccustomed to your heat
this unfamiliar presence
your fingers tracing the line
of my ear

I brush at your hands
too recently
someone else had that pleasure
it is too much

but your fingers trace the line again
your touch persists
asks
and promises

a dozen kisses, more
exactly the way you like them

My Love ❦

I'm afraid to tell you how I see you
in the pink awakenings of the horizon
in the gold stretching and blooming of the sky

I feel the words float to the surface
they press against my lips and then
I feel the beast behind my shoulder

whiskers brush against my neck
the beast holds my throat
as he wraps me in a woolen cloak of fear

I could run to you and offer up my life
my ribs spread wide for an easy reach
let you take my heart between your hands

but what if you too craved meat?
what if your nails scraped behind my heart
pulled it loose from its fleshy wall

and I was left with deathly stillness
the gaping silence of an abandoned house

❦ The one and only poem in this collection written
while the relationship was still in progress.

What You Do to Me

feelings swirl inside my head
like colors

I don't want to see them
if I hold my breath
they slow and stop
I breathe in sips
to keep them still

but when we talk like this
in your car,
the colors begin to move
you bring them up

I can't
hold
my
breath
any
longer

Acrophobia

crawling out on this limb
I can see the ground yawning
hundreds of feet below

before the limb bends
fear drags me down stops me

my forehead pressed to the bark

fingernails digging into wood
marking each minute

shaking
I inch forward
towards you

Step on a Crack

I can't help but feel
like a mother
kneeling, arms outstretched
with a very large toddler

my eyes trace your path as you
charge down the concrete sidewalk
heedless of cracks and bumps
swaying, stumbling
crying boyish tears

I'm always worrying
will I catch you?

Drought

my skin is like a desert
cracks run the length
of my spine
wide open, asking

it has been weeks
since I was last touched

days
are endless

watching you gently touch your lips
to a light stream of water
is almost too much to bear

I turn
my pain
inward

Date Night

going out, I'm like a skeleton
ants crawl along the sidewalk
along the ridges of my bones
beneath old flaps of skin

wind rocks my precarious body
unstable on bird feet
you do not take my hand
not during dinner

no skin to hide behind
I ruin the meal
ants crawling out of my chest
I didn't want to go out

you decide it will be best
if we stay in from now on

Part IV

Resilience

How Could She Stay With Him?

someone took down his wooden signs:
"*High Treason*" and "*Buddhist Prostitutes,*"
only a simple hand-painted
"*Antichrist*" is left

when police took him away
the neighbors came out to watch
drawn like vultures by his shouts

they say he tried to push her down the stairs

she misses him
I know
even as I ask myself
I know

a garden, a household
a life, left to be tended
alone

a space empty of corruption
is still

empty

at first, it does not matter
what you choose
to fill it with

The Third Ex

she tells me her stories
and my lips move along with hers
the rhythm of his words
sounding in my ears again

his 25 texts in one night
how he's changed
how this isn't right
how he'll stop hurting her

he gets in her head and she starts to go back

but she listens to me
she lets me stop her
and I can breathe again

she reads my poems
says I know what this will say before I get past the title

she describes his soul spun of glass
so precious, so easily breakable

and I think oh
why didn't I write that?

with two of us to turn to
a support group of women
who dated the same man
she has recovered faster
she is already embracing life with a fullness
I never had

the second ex
is just beginning to talk about him

I, the first,
cope in my own long and meandering way
feigning strength when what I really have is stamina
to take in more than I should

Locked Inside Your House

it's hard for me not to look,
to see myself as I walk by
I look, because I always do

where you used to live
is a pit the size of four buildings
deep walls of dirt carved in the ground
like God's hand reached down
uprooted your house
and crushed it in His fingers

the destruction of your house
does not stop you
I know you still exist

but as I look at the remains of your house
the haunted feeling I used to have
begins to disappear
something like normality replacing it

my feelings begin to seem less real
existing only in my head
and yours

but that
I hate to admit,
was true all along
it was just a house

to me its decimation
was merited

Oregon Coast

I used to keep
my cliffs and crags
my clay dunes
my grey salt winds
to myself

I brought you
precious dry sands
occasional sunlight
the rest
borne on emptiness

a Florida beach
white diamond sands
I imagine that's what you wanted

I am
gravel and rocks
no amount of erosion
can make me soft

I am a piece of coral in one's shoe
my edges will cut
my winds will chafe

and people will cross mountains
to see my ocean

Gap

I don't remember the five minutes before I left. I remember hearing him say, "How could you do this to me?" and the next memory is walking toward the door, my fragile mind made up. After many years, I asked the deepest corners of my mind, What happened during those five minutes? To my surprise, I received an answer.

I went back in time,

I found old-me, walking alone, on my way to his house. I took my hand and said, "It's going to be okay. You are going to get through this. Hang on. You'll get there one day. I promise."

I went back in time,

I visited myself one night when I was trying to sleep. My horrible futon made my muscles stiff, my old pillow made my neck ache.

"Someday," I told me, "I'll get you a comfortable bed, a better pillow, I promise."

I went back in time to the night that I left.

I walked up to myself, took my hands in mine, looked my

old self in the eye and said, "It's time to go."

"But-But I don't want to," I said, beginning to cry. "I don't want to leave." I took me in my arms and said, "I know."

"I love him! I love him so much," I said.
I kissed my forehead. "I know, but it's time."

I reached into my pocket
and placed a set of old keys gently into my hand
"You have been caged little bird," I said
"These let you out. Fly away."

And so I did

A Better Place

I was frail
like the remains of an old balloon
limp skin
drained of life and buoyancy

you were full of air
so big, you took up the space
that was mine
every inch
no room

leaving you
I'm expanding
my body rises
up

and up
and up
into a sky, so terrible
and breathes

About the Author
Kella Hanna-Wayne

Kella is a disabled, chronically and mentally ill, freelance writer from Eugene, Oregon. In addition to her poetry about abuse, she is the editor, publisher, and main writer for Yopp, a resource-hub dedicated to consolidating the do's and don'ts of social justice.

She specializes in educational writing about civil rights, disability, trauma, and Dissociative Identity Disorder. Her work has been published in the Ms. Magazine blog, The BeZine, Architrave Press, and Uttered Chaos. In her spare time, she loves creating digital art, engaging in lively conversations with her cat Rosa, and working to build a life together with the other alters in her system, The Blueprint System, who are the reason she is still here today.

About the Publisher

www.yoppvoice.com

Yopp is a resource hub that is dedicated to consolidating the do's and don'ts of social justice into clear, overarching principles. It is entirely led and created by marginalized voices.

At Yopp we're dedicated to providing educational material for social justice that emphasizes the individual experience of lived oppression and helps you understand the whole picture instead of memorizing a list of rules.

We know that ending oppression cannot be accomplished by any one person alone. And so, it is our hope is that by creating these resources, we are effectively training hundreds or maybe even thousands of people how to be social activists themselves, thereby amplifying the power available to us.

Note from the Author:

In the summer of 2009, I left a profoundly destructive relationship. That fall, I started using the word "abuse" to describe it. Then, in the winter, I began writing poetry about what happened.

I knew I wanted to write about my experiences earlier than that, especially after I watched Rihanna's interview about her physically abusive relationship with Chris Brown. I thought, "If she can talk about something so personal on national television, I can write a few poems." But it was the recession; I had no job, no money, no permanent place to live. It took a few months to get past just surviving to build enough stability before I could write again.

The first poem I wrote was three pages long and a mess. The second came to me late at night as I tried to think of how to explain why it hurt so much to talk about the relationship. The poem was practically fully formed in my mind, and I had to jump out of bed so I could write it down before I lost it.

For the next several months, poems were always falling out of my head, and I needed constant access to pen and paper to catch them. A few times, I wrote three poems a day, and despite my speed, most of the poems from that first month ended up in the final book. As I continued to process and heal and gain perspective over the years, poems continued to show up that clearly belonged to this story. I even added a poem I had written during the relationship to this collection. It took four years to write them all and eleven years of on and off work to edit and get them to a place where I felt ready to self-publish.

Had I reached that place a few years ago, that would be the end of this author's note. But in the summer of 2020, I was diagnosed with Dissociative Identity Disorder. As a result, the poems I had written years before about my mental state during and after the abuse took on whole new sets of meaning.

I noticed how many poems were about dissociation and how even some described personified symbols who I now know to be alters. I learned that my blacking out on the day I left my abusive relationship was a symptom of DID: amnesia can occur while another alter has control of the body. I learned that AJ, one of my alters and most important person in my life, had made the decision to leave. She did the very thing that I could not and saved us all as a result. I learned this a full seven years after I wrote the poem "Gap" which tells the story of "me" visiting myself and convincing me to leave the relationship.

I don't think I could've finished this book without first knowing about my system of alters, who helped keep me alive before, during, and after the abuse. I could not have done the final writing and editing of the poems without Amy, Jessica, and Hazel. I could not have done the illustration and design without AJ and Billie. Finally, I could not have decided to publish without the help of Wendy and Holly. I owe everything to them and everyone else in the system, and I am so grateful to have the opportunity for us to share this book with you.

We hope that if you have experienced or witnessed abuse, these poems will give you better insight into yourself and others about what happened, why it happened, and what comes next.

Help Is Available

If you believe you may be in danger or suspect your relationship may be abusive, please consider visiting **TheHotline.org**. Or call:

1-800-799-7233

To talk to someone about getting you support and help catered to your specific situation.